Camping it up!
On the
Cleveland Way

Ray and Pauline Moody

Rockumentarypress

Contents

Walkers of the 1950s on the Cleveland Way Trail

Foreword

After completing the Coast-to-Coast Walk twice, we felt too embarrassed to do it again for a while, so we looked around for another long-distance trek to take on.

Having already walked over the Cleveland Hills on both the Coast-to-Coast Walk and the Lyke Wake Walk, and living in North Yorkshire, it seemed that the natural thing to do next was to hike the Cleveland Way.

Living at the end of the walk in Filey, I think we had initially undervalued it. But just like the Coast-to-Coast, we discovered it to be a great walk, having its own quiet personality.

Whilst it's certainly not as popular as the Coast-to-Coast walk, and you're unlikely to come across hordes of walkers doing it, you will appreciate the Cleveland Way for having many of its own qualities.

We've now done the walk many times and have enjoyed every adventure.

Ray and Pauline Moody

1

Campsites on the

Cleveland Way

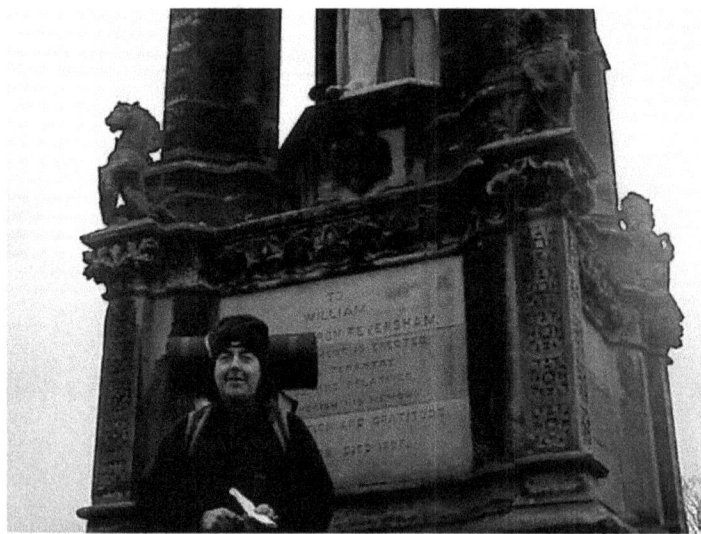

The start at the monument in Helmsley

CAMPSITES ON THE CLEVELAND WAY

Helmsley to Filey

Bungdale Head Farm Camping

Scawton, Thirsk, YO7 2HH

Ten minutes from the main trail:

Tel: 01439 770589

Mobile: 07792 790434

Email: sm.foster@hotmail.co.uk

Website: www.bungdaleheadcamping.co.uk/

Camping Details:

The campsite is about three miles from Helmsley. Cost £10 per person. The site includes a toilet block with hot and cold water and washbasins. Camping on a working farm with great views. After passing by Rievaulx Abbey and over Rievaulx Bridge, you continue on along the road. Eventually, the Cleveland Way turns off to the right to leave it. Instead of following the trail and leaving the road by going through the gate, continue on along the road for a few more minutes. The campsite is off to your left. Follow the farm trod down to it and retrace your steps in the morning.

High Paradise Farm

Boltby, Thirsk, North Yorkshire, YO7 2HT

On route: You pass through it on the walk.

Tel: 01845 537353

Mobile: 07739 498255

Email: info@highparadise.co.uk

Website: www.highparadise.co.uk/camping.html

Camping Details: Cost £10 per person, per night. Basic camping, hot and cold water, toilet block. shower facility, outdoor kitchen with hot water. No need to book. Just turn up before 5pm and go to the tearoom. Text mobile 07739498255 to let them know that you are coming.

Cote Ghyll Caravan & Camping Park

Osmotherley, North Yorkshire, DL6 3AH

Slightly off route: by half a mile

OS Grid Ref: 459 979

Tel: 01609 883425

Email: hills@coteghyll.com

Website: https://coteghyll.campmanager.com

Camping Details: £17.00 per person

A commercial campsite, quite expensive. Facilities include hot water, toilets, and a very clean shower block. You must book in advance. You need to mention that you're on the Cleveland Way. Arriving Monday to Thursday is best.

Lord Stones Country Park

Lord Stones, Carlton Bank, Chop Gate, North Yorkshire, TS9 7JH

Tel: 01642 778482

Email: info@lordstones.com

Website: https://lordstones.com/

Camping Details: Cost for one person, £25.00. Shower and toilet facilities. Great situation overlooking the Cleveland Plain. Restaurant close by.

Beakhills Farm

Cringle Moor, Chop Gate, Middlesborough, TS9 7JJ

Email: booking@beakhillsfarm.co.uk

Website: https://www.beakhillsfarm.co.uk

Tel: 01642 778371

Grid Ref: 545 024

Camping Details:

To be found after the Lord Stones. Pass the Falconer Seat and Cringle Moor, then find it half-a-mile off route. Follow sign pointing to the farm, which you'll see before you get to the Wainstones. Warm showers and toilet.

Cost only £10 per person. Just turn up.

Great Broughton

Jet Miners Inn, High Street, Great Broughton, TS9 7ES

Off Route: Two and a half miles off-route (plus return in the morning) turn left at Clay Bank Top and follow the road.

Tel: 01642 712642

Mobile 07810118590

Camping Details: £10 per person. Modern Toilets and shower block. The Bay Horse pub in Great Broughton does the best homemade Vegetable Lasagne in the whole of Yorkshire.

Kildale

Park Farm, Kildale, North Yorkshire, Y021 2RN

On Route:

Tel: 01642 722847

Email: barnandcamping@kildalebarn.co.uk

Camping Details: £10 per person, per night. Facilities include the use of a fridge, microwave, toaster, kettle and electric points. Shared shower (£1) and toilet facilities. Hot and cold water available. A camping barn is also available at £12 per person, per night. £1 coins required for electric meters. A byre is also available at £15 per person for a bit more luxury. Sleeps up to five.

Boosbeck
Margrove Park Caravan Site
Margrove, Boosbeck, TS12 3BZ
Tel: 01287 653616
Email: margrovepark@btconnect.com
Camping Details: £10 per person, per night.
Comfortable toilet and washroom block with hot
water. Instead of crossing the road to the Fox and
Hounds pub at Slapewath, turn right and cross the
road. After about 5 minutes walking, turn left down
the road signposted Margrove Park and Lingdale.
After a quarter of a mile, turn right into campsite.
Only accepts campers on the Cleveland Way

Serenity Camping
High St, Hinderwell, Whitby, North Yorkshire,
TS13 5JH
Tel: 01947 841122
Off route:
Camping Details:
This site is just over a mile away from
Runswick Bay. But you can catch the X4 bus to
it from Runswick Bay, if you can't get in at the
campsite there. Camping costs £28 for two
sharing a tent.

Runswick Bay

Runswick Bay Caravan & Camping Park
Hinderwell Lane, Runswick Bay,
North Yorkshire, TS13 5HR
Tel: 01947 840997
Camping Details: Quite expensive, £30 for two sharing tent for one night There is normally a two-night stay required, so you must mention that you can only spend one night there as you're doing the Cleveland Way. Toilet block with hot water and showers.

Whitby

High Straggleton Farm, Sandsend Road, Whitby, North Yorkshire, TS21 3SR
Tel: 01947 602373
On route:
OS Grid Ref: NZ878114
Camping Details: There isn't a campsite actually situated in Whitby, and this campsite is on the right-hand side of the Sandsend Road, opposite the golf course, just before you make your way into the town. Toilet and shower block available.

Robin Hood's Bay

Hook's House Farm, Whitby Road, Robin Hood's Bay

Tel: 01947 880283

OS Grid Ref: 946058

Website: www.hookshousefarm.co.uk

Camping Details: £25 per tent. Showers, toilets, pot washing sinks available. Mention that you're on the Cleveland Way, because usually customers have to stay at the site for a minimum of a two-nights. This seems to be the policy along the East Coast. Great views of the bay.

Snow on the Hambleton Hills

Middlewood Farm Holiday Park

Middlewood Farm Holiday Park,
Robin Hood's Bay, North Yorkshire,
YO22 4UF

Tel: 01947 880414

Email: info@middlewoodfarm.com

Camping Details:

Ten minutes' walk from Robin Hood's Bay's main street. You can get to it from the bottom of the long winding street near the seafront. Look out for the fish and chip shop, which you'll find down a alleyway. Going down it, turn right at the end of the passage.

The rising path will eventually take you to the site. On the way, you cross over Robin Hood's Bay old railway line. The site has a laundry room complete with washer, dryer and iron. Showers and hot water are also available. There is also an undercover dish washing area. Cost varies, depending on the month. It is usually £25 person. Some dates require a minimum two-night stay. So, inform them that you are doing the Cleveland Way.

Ravenscar

Bent Rigg Farm

Ravenscar, Scarborough, North Yorkshire,
YO13 0NG

Tel: 01723 870475

Camping Details:

Basic facilities. £10 per person. Toilet.

Scarborough

Scalby Manor Touring Caravans and Camping Park

Burniston Road, Scarborough, North Yorkshire,
YO13 0DA

Tel: 01723 366212

Camping Details: You pass a sign on the cliff top path about half a mile before you get to Scalby Mills at the end of the cliffs. The sign points the way to Helmsley, and is the start of the Tabular Hills Walk. Follow the path through a couple of fields and after about 10 minutes you'll come out onto a road. The gate to the campsite is directly opposite. It's a large commercial site, but Backpackers are charged £12 per night. Small shop, restaurant and Pub available on site.

Filey

Filey Brigg Touring Caravan Park
Filey YO14 9ET
Tel: 01723 513852
Camping Details: Site on the cliff top above Filey Brigg.

Ryedale

2

Planning the Walk

Planning the Journey
Day 1: Helmsley to High Paradise
13 miles

Although there is a slow, gradual climb from Helmsley to Sutton Bank, the first day of the Cleveland Way is relatively easy and provides a gentle introduction to the walk. You are walking across the Rye Valley. This section involves both road and forestry walking. Highlights of this section of the Way include Rievaulx Abbey, the views from Sutton Bank, and looking down on Lake Gormire. From Sutton Bank, you simply follow the escarpment edge until you reach High Paradise Farm. The walking is on the same level, and no route finding is required. On a clear day, the views from the edge over the Yorkshire Plain are sensational.

There would normally be no sense in stopping before you get to High Paradise Farm, as there now isn't another campsite directly on route during this first section of the walk.

But if you've arrived in Helmsley late, then you can walk the three miles to the Bungdale Head campsite, which is a mile or so past Rievaulx Abbey and about 10 minutes after where you would normally turn off towards the Nettledale ponds.

Continuing to follow the road beyond Rievaulx Abbey, you will arrive at a place on your right where the Cleveland Way turns off through a gate. Instead of turning off, you need to continue on down the road. After about five minutes, you'll come to a narrow farm road on your left, which leads to the campsite. Camping there for the evening will leave you with a long 19-mile journey to Osmotherley or a short 12-mile day to High Paradise Farm the following day.

Sutton Bank

Day 2: High Paradise to Osmotherley

8 miles

Shortly after leaving High Paradise Farm, you turn onto an ancient drover's road. On reaching a forest, you pass through the edge of it. It doesn't last long, and you soon come out at a gate and a stone known as the Steeple Cross.

The main part of the day is now before you. You will spend the next two hours walking across high-level moorland. If the weather is fine, it's easy walking, and you can see the plateau of Black Hambleton rising up in the distance.

Walking alongside a wall, it seems to take an age before you turn round it and pass over Black Hambleton. Making your way down to a road, you walk alongside the reservoir of Oakdale, before sauntering your way down country lanes and into Osmotherley.

Osmotherley probably has the cleanest campsite on the whole route, but you need to book in advance because on weekends it gets full.

If it is, then you will need to walk on a further five miles to the Lord Stones at Carlton Bank, where there is plenty of expensive camping available, or push on to Beakhills Farm, which is much cheaper.

Day 3: Osmotherley to Great Broughton

13 miles

The Cleveland Hills are the jewel in the crown of the Cleveland Way. Also forming part of the Lyke Wake Walk and the Coast-to-Coast Walk, they are strenuous but sensational.

You begin the day by making your way up to the trig point on Beacon Hill. You can either follow the signposted route or take a shortcut via the tarmacked BT road. This will bring you out at the satellite station on Beacon Hill, just a short distance away from the trig point. From the top of Beacon Hill, you begin three hours of undulation as you climb over the switchback of the Cleveland Hills. The only place you could get lost on today's journey is in the afforested plantation of Coalmire. But if you stick to the path close to the edge of the wood, you won't go off on any false trails.

It's twelve miles over the Cleveland Hills to Clay Bank Top and a further two miles down the road to Great Broughton if you're using the campsite there. But if you're a good walker, it's quite possible to continue on to Kildale, which will make it a 20-mile day. We've done it many times wearing full backpacks. But after climbing the

Cleveland hills, it does feel like a very long day. This is especially so after leaving Bloworth Crossing, as the path across the moors to Kildale seems to go on and on, and you're guaranteed to arrive there exhausted.

But if you're short of time and considering walking all the way to Kildale, then to speed things up and to conserve your energy, after the Lord Stones Cafe, instead of climbing up to the Falconer Seat, take the lower-level path and follow it all the way along to Clay Bank Top. But you can also later leave it if you wish to visit the Wainstones and rejoin the higher-level route. As you near the Wainstones, climb over a stile and follow a short path up to them. These really are worth a visit.

Breaking the trip at the Jet Miners Inn in Great Broughton gives you both a nice campsite and a choice of pubs. If you're vegetarian, they do a great homemade 'veg lag' at the Bay Horse. It really is tasty, and you certainly get a plate full. Make the most of it, as there isn't a pub in Kildale.

Day 4: Great Broughton to Kildale
11 miles

From Great Broughton, it's two miles down the road to Hasty Bank and nine miles across the moor to Kildale. But after the initial climb up onto Urra Moor, which lasts for about thirty minutes, the walking is relatively flat on easy paths and only slightly uphill. You'll soon arrive at the former track-bed of the old ironstone railway line and follow it along to Bloworth Crossing.

It's here that you part company with Coast-to-Coast walkers, who will continue on along the track to the Lion Inn on Blakey Ridge. Cleveland Way walkers turn off at Bloworth Crossing for Kildale. It really is a trek across the moors, and Tidy Brown Hill always seems a long time in coming. If you've already climbed the Cleveland Hills today, you'll arrive at Kildale feeling quite spent.

We've both camped and used the bunk barn at Kildale and have spent many an evening there listening to radio programmes coming over the airwaves from Newcastle. There is a coin-operated electric meter in the barn, and we would sit cosily together around a one-bar electric fire. Sheer luxury after our nights in the tent. Rather than sleeping directly on the mattresses provided, Pauline would insist that we put our tent up on top of one of them. This was her way of ensuring that we didn't get any rats crawling over us during the night!

On the way to Boosbeck

Day 5: Kildale to Margrove Park, Boosbeck
12 miles

Despite not now having a pub or shop, Kildale has its own railway station, a handy escape route, where you can catch a train to Whitby if needed.

Passing the railway station, you climb up a steep road before turning off for the Captain Cook monument.

Leaving it, you go downhill to meet a road and then immediately begin a climb back up the other side. Shortly, a Cleveland Hill that's got separated from the rest will appear.

Roseberry Topping is Yorkshire's Matterhorn, and it's well worth leaving your backpack at the bottom of the hill to quickly climb it. Beyond Roseberry Topping, you head off across the moors for Guisborough Woods.

When we first walked through them, they were so dense that it was easy to get lost. But in recent years, many of the trees have been cut back or felled, and the woods now seem much friendlier and much less of a remote place.

Coming out of the trees at Slapewath, you normally head off across the road towards the Fox and Hounds pub on your left, where the Cleveland

Way continues. But if you're staying at the Margrove Park campsite, then you turn right down the road before turning left towards Boosbeck, following the road down to the campsite.

This campsite has a lovely warm, clean, immaculate toilet block. But the owners of the site always seem to direct you to hide your tent away from the main caravan pitches. It's as though they're ashamed of backpackers being on view!

Day 6: Boosbeck to Runswick Bay
16 miles

From the Margrove Park campsite, you can retrace your steps back to the Fox and Hounds pub and rejoin the Cleveland Way route, or you can simply follow the road down into Boosbeck, where you'll find some small grocery stores. Continuing to follow the road, you can re-join the Cleveland Way route at Skelton. Here you turn off to your right and follow a long, raised passageway that soon takes you into the settlement of Skelton Green.

There are even more local shops here. But you're now not far from Saltburn. So, you quickly pass by them and make your way through a housing estate.

Beyond the council housing, you follow a path across a field to a newly built private housing development.

Where the houses are situated, a few years ago there was a dark, dank, overgrown wood. The Cleveland Way went through it. The wood was often frequented by local youths who used to hang about in the semi-gloom of the closely compacted bushes and trees. Carrying a video camera, I always felt a bit wary.

It is so much nicer now as you walk through the new houses. Beyond them, you walk alongside a field until coming to an opening into a wood. Descending down to a stream, you follow a path alongside it. Cross over the stream via a metal bridge close to a huge Victorian railway viaduct. Once over the bridge, you are in Saltburn Valley Gardens proper. Following the paths, you're gradually walking into the heart of Saltburn.

We used to do a long 28-mile day from Kildale to Staithes and would try to regain some of our energy in Saltburn by treating ourselves to toasted sandwiches in a local café. We would also stock up on a few goodies at Sainsbury's supermarket.

With your shopping over with, head for the seafront. After walking along the promenade for a short distance, turn right at the Ship Inn, and begin the climb out of Saltburn via the steep steps climbing up the cliffside. Once on top of the cliff, you'll soon be looking out over Saltburn and at the Victorian pier on the seafront.

Walking over the cliff top, you meet up with many local dog walkers. You'll also pass by several memorial plaques on the cliff edge. These indicate where people have either fallen or jumped to their death. All of the plaques give the telephone number of the Samaritans.

As the cliff climbs steadily higher, there are views back to a distinctive row of Saltburn's fine Victorian terraced houses, which stay in view for quite a while.

Soon you reach an industrial railway line. The track between the edge of the cliff and the railway line becomes much narrower for a while. There are fine views down to the sea and the rocky bottom of the cliff. Soon afterwards, you arrive at what appears to be a huge, metal, lucky charm bracelet. It stands on one of the cliff-top hillocks. As a kind of ritual, we always clang each of the lucky charms together.

As we near Skinningrove, a long series of wooden steps takes us down to the beach. The trick is to try to stay off the sand for as long as possible by following the path hidden amongst the dunes. But eventually, you have to leave them and go down onto the sand. Walking on the sand is heavy going, but from there, you make your way towards the concrete jetty.

Leaving the beach, you follow a wide gravel track as it takes you towards Skinningrove's seafront terraced houses. In recent years, the place has been tidied up and seems to be slowly moving away from its one-time image of being a declining fishing village, and it is now attracting many more visitors.

There is claimed to a shop and a fish and chip shop somewhere up there in the village, but we have never had the strength to go and look for it.

Passing a public toilet block, to leave Skinningrove, you turn left and cross a bridge over a stream. Just beyond some old wooden sheds, there is a huge climb up the cliffside via a long series of high steps. I can never get beyond halfway up these steps without resting, but the views are sensational.

Back on the cliff top, we're now heading towards Boulby Cliff, and the steadily rising path takes us inland for a short while.

Passing through some isolated farm cottages with fine views out to sea, we commence the climb up Boulby Cliff. The ascent is steady and doesn't seem as bad as it first looks. Gradually, we gain height and reach the top edge of the cliff. Here, some huge rocky outcrops jut out above the North Sea.   If you look carefully at the outcrop, you can spot the place where a heartbroken husband has chiselled a love letter to his wife into the rock.

The whole length of the cliffs from Saltburn to Scarborough is adorned with benches dedicated to loved ones who once walked this way. We often stop to read them. This is the way people are remembered and, for a moment, are brought back to mind.

The top of Boulby Cliff can easily be spotted by looking for the large television aerial, which stands in a field by the side of the trail.

Once beyond it, the path begins to drop down. descending the cliff. As the path flattens out you head towards a row of cottages, which you will pass.

One of these cottages was once the home of the legendary 'Walkers Halt,' a cliff-top café. A place you could drop into at any time of the day or night and enjoy a cup of tea and a snack.

Beyond Boltby Cliff, there is a straight track across a field that eventually arrives at Staithes. But it's a long mile. On the way you will pass a memorial seat dedicated to the former couple who ran the Walker's Halt.

We frequently used to be climbing over Boulby Cliff in the semi-gloom, having walked all the way from Kildale. It was often after 7 o'clock at night, and it was such a relief to be able to get off our feet at the Walker's Halt for half-an-hour before the final long mile into Staithes and the former campsite at Trig Point 49.

Arriving at seafaring Staithes at around 8 o'clock on an evening, we'd often walk up its dark main street in the misty gloom. Passing a building that was once a Bethel (a sailor's chapel and hostel) I always thought of Robert Louis Stevenson's book 'Kidnapped,' and it was easy to imagine that the press-gang was waiting just around the corner.

There are one or two friendly pubs in Staithes, and one of them holds a quiz night every Wednesday evening.

But now there isn't a campsite in the village, and the nearest one is a further three miles away along the cliff at Runswick Bay. But after climbing out of Staithes, apart from one further steep climb, the walking along the cliff is relatively flat, and you soon arrive at the hamlet of Runswick Bay.

If you can't manage the extra three miles today, then you can ascend the steep hill out of Staithes and, at the bus shelter on the main road, catch the X4 Whitby/Saltburn bus to the campsite at Runswick Bay or to the campsite at Hinderwell. Simply return by bus in the morning. In the summer months these buses run every half hour. In the winter months they run every hour.

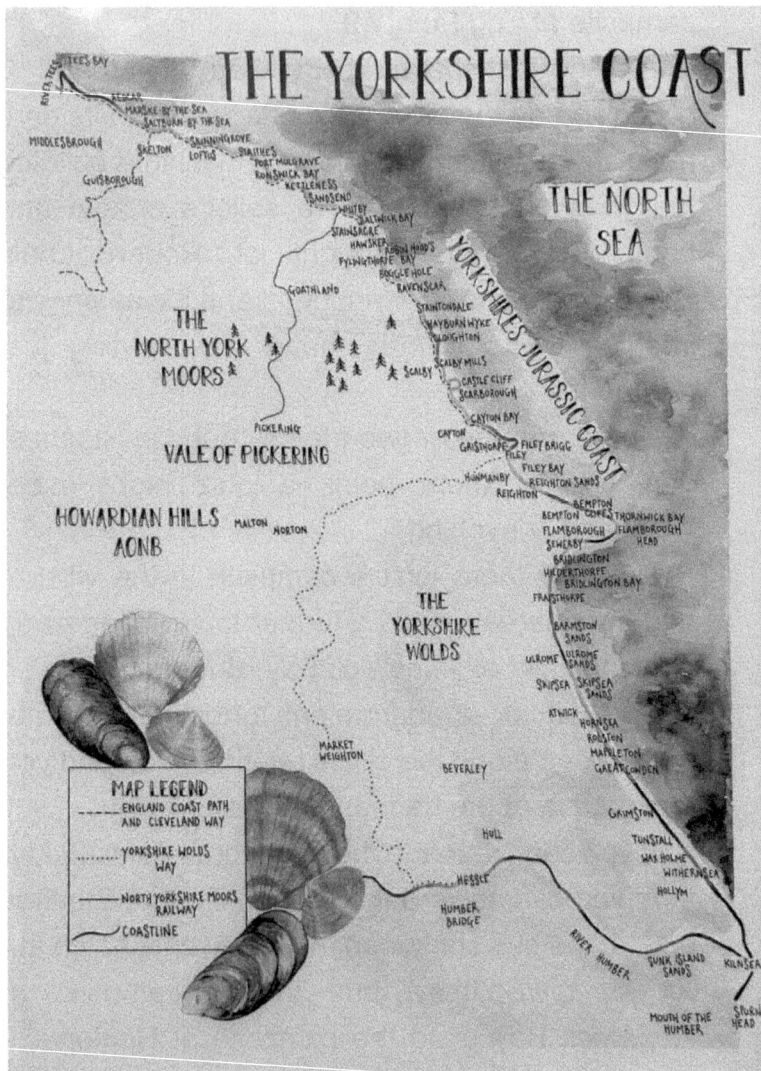

THE YORKSHIRE COAST

THE NORTH SEA

THE NORTH YORK MOORS

VALE OF PICKERING

HOWARDIAN HILLS AONB

THE YORKSHIRE WOLDS

MAP LEGEND
- ENGLAND COAST PATH AND CLEVELAND WAY
- YORKSHIRE WOLDS WAY
- NORTH YORKSHIRE MOORS RAILWAY
- COASTLINE

Map by Vicki Vis showing all of the small settlements you will pass as you make your way down the coast.

Day 7: Runswick Bay to Robin Hood's Bay
16 miles

As you walk across the sand at Runswick Bay, the scene is glorious, a mini paradise. You're heading for a ravine at the far end of the beach and hoping that the tide won't come in before you get there.

On arriving at this gash in the cliffside, turn off down it and walk alongside a beck before going over a wooden bridge. You then begin a steep climb back up to the cliff top. It always seems like a long way up. Back on the cliff top, this is the place where a grass snake once sidewinded its way over my boot.

Following the clifftop path, you eventually arrive on what was once the old Scarborough to Whitby railway line. Climbing down a serious series of steep ladder steps, you eventually arrive down near the entrance to the old railway tunnel. After admiring it, you now walk on the cinder track of the old railway line. The views down to the sea and towards Whitby are spectacular. What a journey it must have been to travel by train along this coastline. The cinder track turns a corner, and we're heading towards Sandsend and pass by its old railway station.

It seems like a long way in from Sandsend to Whitby, but at least you know that there is the possibility of refreshments at the end of it. Walking down the road towards Whitby Golf Course, you can visit several cafes and a grocery store. Passing by the golf course, you eventually turn off down a thoroughfare towards the sea. As you pass under a very distinct bridge, which enables golfers to get from one side of the golf course to the other, watch out for flying golf balls. Passing rows of houses and more memorial seats, you arrive on Whitby promenade and the start of the crowds. As you approach the Whalebone arch, turn right and make your way down a narrow street into the town centre.

After shopping, cross over the harbour bridge and make your way towards the infamous series of stone steps that lead up to Whitby Abbey. After climbing the steps, you pass through a churchyard and by the ruins of the abbey and arrive back on the cliff top.

Following the path along the cliff edge, you come to a caravan park. You used to be able to use the loos here, but now they are kept securely locked. So, if you're desperate, you'll have to wait for someone to go in or come out! There is also a camp shop here, albeit expensive, but if you're in need of refreshments, then it's worth a visit.

Beyond the caravan park, looking down from the cliffs, you see the towering, isolated, black rock known as The Nab. It looks like the turret of a submarine rising out of the water. I would love to shin down the cliffs with a bucket of white gloss and paint the letters U2 on it. It really does look like a submarine surfacing through the waves.

Soon you'll pass the lighthouse and the foghorn station. I'm always frightened that someone might decide to test the horns as we pass.

After a climb up from the lighthouse, we arrive at Hawsker. This is the place where the Coast-to-Coast walk comes in and joins the Cleveland Way for three miles. Beyond it there is a straightforward walk along a cliff-top path until it bends its way into Robin Hood's Bay.

Upon arriving, there, you have a choice of two campsites. Turn right at the grounds of the former railway station and walk uphill to Hook's End Farm. It's a nice place to stay. You can enjoy panoramic views of Robin Hood's Bay from the campsite.

There is a food store on the main road before you make your way down the long, winding street to the sea. Close to the slipway at the bottom, there is a fish and chip shop. But it cooks in animal fats. Vegetarian walkers, however, can still enjoy a plate of chips. You can purchase them at the Bay Hotel, where they are cooked in vegetable oil.

In the forest after the Drovers Road

Day 8: Robin Hood's Bay to Scarborough
16 miles

Climbing out of Robin Hood's Bay, you arrive back on the cliff top. The path is easy to follow, and you soon arrive at Boggle Hole Youth Hostel. Beyond it, you make your way to Ravenscar, the end of the Lyke Wake Walk, but there is some steep climbing before you reach it.

A National Trust Centre is situated at Ravenscar, where you can buy refreshments. I once set off from Robin Hood's Bay without any water and was so dehydrated by the time I got to Ravenscar that I was thankful to be able to buy a bottle there.

Ravenscar is the seaside village that never took off, mainly because what bit of beach it has is situated at the bottom of a cliff.

You pass the grand Ravenhall Hotel, where you can call in for a pint. At the end of one particular Lyke Wake Walk, we did this on a tremendously hot day, and I enjoyed the best pint of bitter shandy I have ever tasted.

Beyond Ravenscar, you pass by the strange silent remains of some wartime radar buildings.

Eventually, the walk along the cliff top takes you down into the picturesque Hayburn Wyke. A place that was particularly popular in the 1920s when visitors could arrive here by train. It is easy to get lost here as you attempt to climb out of the wood.

You can see the castle at Scarborough from quite a distance, but it's still a trek to get to it. Just before you're about to leave the cliff and go down to the northern edge of Scarborough's promenade at Scalby Mills, you pass the sign for the start of the Tabular Hills walk. If you're staying at the campsite in Scarborough, you should follow the sign across the field, and within five minutes, it will bring you out at the campsite. There are regular buses to be had here that will take you down into the heart of Scarborough.

Day 9: Scarborough to Filey
12 miles

The walk along the promenade in Scarborough goes on for miles. Just following the road through North Bay alone is probably about two miles long. When you're finally level with the castle, you're still less than halfway along Scarborough's seafront. But eventually you'll arrive at the plethora of amusement arcades on the South Bay.

If you need provisions, you should climb up one of the side streets, such as Bland's Cliff, and do your shopping in town before rejoining the route.

Continuing to follow the path along the seafront, you eventually leave the amusement arcades behind and pass beneath the Grand Hotel. You're now heading towards Scarborough's Spa Theatre, close to where you climb up through the Italian Gardens and follow the road past numerous hotels before turning left down one of the last streets as you leave Scarborough. It will take you to a quiet path running along the cliff edge, and you'll leave behind the busy bustle of England's first seaside resort.

Once on the path, it will lead you above the sands of Cayton Bay and then through a caravan park. Back on the cliff edge, the path rises as it takes you past yet another caravan site.

Leaving the caravans behind, you continue along the clifftop path and soon see the roof of St. Oswald's Church in Filey in the distance. As you keep along the path, you'll see the cliff top stretching off to the left. This is Filey Brigg. Just at the start of the Brigg, there is a stone seat marking the end of the Cleveland Way. Sitting down on it, you can relax and relive the journey you've just completed.

Filey's glorious beach lies below you, and after walking across the edge of the Country Park, you can follow the steps down to it and the promenade before climbing up the main street into the town. If you're camping, you should first book a pitch here on the clifftop.

The great thing about Filey is that it has a railway station. From early morning until nine o'clock on an evening, you can catch a train to Hull, Doncaster, Sheffield, York, and Leeds. So, if you've had enough of camping, you can head-off home. And if you've left your tent at the campsite at Scarborough (to save you from having to carry your backpack all the way to Filey) then you catch a bus or train back there.

3

Walking Itineraries

Walking Itinerary - 9 Days

Day 1
Helmsley to High Paradise
13 miles

Day 2
High Paradise to Osmotherley
8 miles

Day 3
Osmotherley – Great Broughton
13 miles

Day 4
Great Broughton- Kildale
11.3 miles

Day 5
Kildale to Margrove Park
12 miles

Day 6
Margrove Park – Runswick Bay
16 miles

Day 7
Runswick Bay to Robin Hood's Bay
17 miles

Day 8
Robin Hood's Bay to Scarborough
15 miles

Day 9
Scarborough to Filey
11 miles

Details
When you're backpacking the Cleveland Way, unless you're planning to wild camp, you need to plan your days so that you'll arrive at the next available campsite. This needs to be within a reasonable day's walking distance, so your stopping places will be governed by this.

Walking Itinerary - 8 Days

Day 1
Helmsley to High Paradise
14 miles

Day 2
High Paradise to Osmotherley
8 miles

Day 3
Osmotherley to Kildale
20 miles

Day 4
Kildale to Margrove Park
12 miles

Day 5
Margrove Park to Runswick Bay
17 miles

Day 6
Runswick Bay to Robin Hood's Bay
14 miles

Day 7
Robin Hood's Bay – Scarborough
15 miles

Day 8
Scarborough to Filey
11 miles

Details
The route includes one really hard day, Osmotherley to Kildale. Once you've arrived at Clay Bank Top, there is a steep climb up onto Urra Moor. But within an hour you should find the walking easy. Going on auto-pilot, you follow a well-defined path over the moor before climbing up onto the track-bed of the old ironstone railway line and then leave it at Bloworth Crossing to follow a long trek across the moors to Kildale.

Walking Itinerary - 10 Days

Day 1
Helmsley – Bungdale Head Farm
3.5 miles

Day 2
Bungdale Head Farm to High Paradise
9 miles

Day 3
High Paradise to Osmotherley
8 miles

Day 4
Osmotherley – Great Broughton
13 Miles

Day 5
Great Broughton- Kildale
11.3 miles

Day 6
Kildale to Margrove Park
12 miles

Day 7

Margrove Park – Runswick Bay

17 miles

Day 8

Runswick Bay to Robin Hood's Bay

14 miles

Day 9

Robin Hood's Bay to Scarborough

15 miles

Day 10

Scarborough to Filey

11 miles

Walking Itinerary - 8 Days

Day 1
Helmsley – Bungdale Head Farm
3 miles

Day 2
Bungdale Head Farm to Osmotherley
18 miles

Day 3
Osmotherley to Kildale
20 miles

Day 4
Kildale to Margrove Park
12 miles

Day 5
Margrove Park to Runswick Bay
17 miles

Day 6
Runswick Bay to Robin Hood's Bay
14 miles

Day 7
Robin Hood's Bay to Scarborough
14 miles

Day 8
Scarborough to Filey
11 miles

Walking Itinerary - 7 Days

Day 1
Helmsley to Osmotherley
21 miles

Day 2
Osmotherley to Kildale
20 miles

Day 3
Kildale to Margrove Park
12 miles

Day 4
Margrove Park to Runswick Bay
17 miles

Day 5
Runswick Bay to Robin Hood's Bay
14 miles

Day 6
Robin Hood's Bay – Scarborough
14 miles

Day 7
Scarborough to Filey
11 miles

Details
Two hard days, Helmsley to Osmotherley and Osmotherley to Kildale. After this the walk settles down nicely. You would need to set off from Helmsley by 0900 hrs. at the latest, if you're to get to Osmotherley by teatime.

Backwards in 9 days

Day 1
Filey to Scarborough
10 miles

Day 2
Scarborough to Robin Hood's Bay
14 miles

Day 3
Robin Hood's Bay to Runswick Bay
14 miles

Day 4
Runswick Bay to Margrove Park
17 miles

Day 5
Margrove Park to Kildale
12 miles

Day 6
Kildale to Great Broughton
11.3 miles

Day 7

Great Broughton to Osmotherley

13 miles

Day 8

Osmotherley to High Paradise

8 miles

Day 9

High Paradise to Helmsley

14 miles

Details

On a weekend in the summer, there are occasional buses from Sutton Bank to Scarborough.

4

Food and Shops

Shops and Food

We usually take two to three days' basic food rations with us. This is food which you can buy in packets, such as various flavours of packet pasta, mashed potato, Beanfeast, croutons, breakfast cereals, and soup. We supplement this with items of food we buy at the shops we come across along the way.

Helmsley

The small Co-op store has a range of food items. A cash machine is available in the market square.

Sutton Bank Tourism Centre

You can stop off here for coffee, cake, and a toilet break. Food and drink items are quite expensive.

High Paradise

Café here with drinks and eats. Closes at 3 pm.

Osmotherley

There is a small Village store in Osmotherley opposite the campsite. Plenty of pubs.

Carlton Bank (Lord Stones)

As you climb down from Carlton Bank, you'll see some   parked cars. Make your way towards them and you'll find the Lord Stones restaurant. The original Lord Stones was the finest cafe on the whole route, an oasis in the metaphorical desert of the Cleveland Hills, and you'd arrive at it from Osmotherley just when you're feeling like taking your first break of the day. A new, more upmarket restaurant has now taken its place. But it's still a good place to stop for a break, and it could provide you with the energy you'll need for your climb up to the Falconer Seat.

Great Broughton

Two pubs, no village store.

Kildale

Café, no pub, and no shop. But there is a railway station. Trains run from about 1300 hrs to either Middlesbrough or Whitby.

Boosbeck

Small shops in Boosbeck, if you take the road route to Skelton rather than retrace your footsteps back to the Fox and Hounds at Slapewath.

Skelton/Skelton Green
Small shops in Skelton and Skelton Green.

Saltburn-on-Sea
Plenty of shops, a large Sainsbury supermarket, bakeries, fish and chips shops, and cafes. Restock your supplies here. Cash machines are also available, and there is a railway station and buses from here to Whitby.

Skinningrove
Fish and chip shop, store and Post Office.

Staithes
Coop Store and fish and chip shop up past the hill as you climb out of Staithes.

Sandsend
Cafes, no shop.

Whitby
Large Coop supermarket in the town centre, but Whitby also has lots of smaller shops with discounted food. Plenty of fish and chip shops, bakeries, etc. Last chance for a cash machine before Scarborough. Restock your supplies.

Robin Hood's Bay

Robin Hood's Bay has a village store, fish and chip shop, and sweet shop. You can also purchase a plate of chips in the Bay Hotel where they are cooked in vegetable oil. The village store is expensive but sells lots of goodies. The fish and chip shop can be found down at the bottom of the long, winding street which leads to the sea. Sadly. it cooks in animal fats. Enjoy a coffee in the Victoria Hotel. No cash machine in RHB.

Ravenscar

National Trust shop sells hot and cold drinks, cakes and sweets.

Scarborough

Lots of shops in Scarborough including Tesco, Aldi, Herons. Bakeries, MacDonald's, and lots of fish and chips shops. Banks, cash machines and train station available.

Filey

Tesco, Heron's, Spar, Coupland's Bakery. Fish and chip shops, cash machines, buses and train station available.

5

A Few Tips

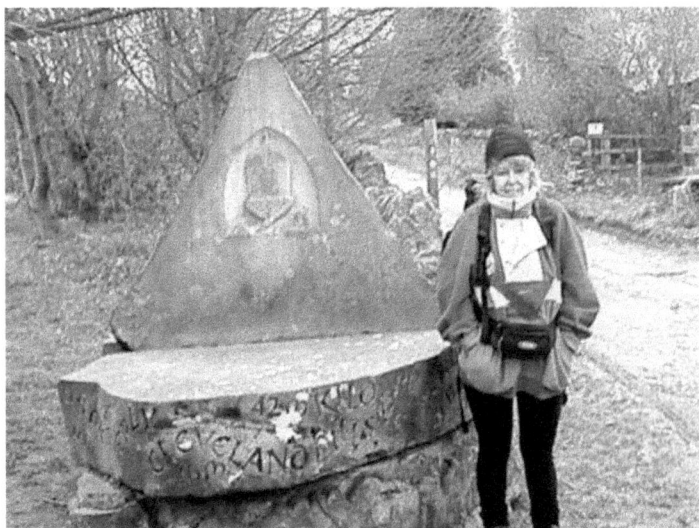

The official Start of the Cleveland Way

A few Tips

Do I need to book in advance at the campsites?

For most of them, you don't usually have to book in advance and can just turn up. But it's best to book in at the Cote Gylle campsite at Osmotherley if you want to be guaranteed a pitch. But the site will charge you in advance on your debit card,

Don't wear new boots. If you have bought some, especially for the trip, make sure that you have walked around in them for a while before you start the walk.

Buy a tent that weighs under 2.5 kg. Usually, tents that are lighter than this cost a couple of hundred pounds. But check out the weight of the tents in the Argos catalogue or at Millets, where you can find tents for as little as £50, which weigh about 2.4 kg and do the job. I always count out the exact number of tent pegs needed, carrying just two spares, and I leave the rest at home. You can also buy some lightweight aluminium tent pegs to replace the heavier ones you probably got with the tent.

Timing

Aim to set off each day at 8.30 hrs (even if slightly late). By doing this, you will be able to spend more time gazing at the sights and resting at your destination. I work on a walking calculation of two miles per hour, which means that when walking a 16-mile day, you are guaranteed to arrive at your destination within 8 hours. This timing allows for any breaks you may take along the way. You simply adjust your estimated time of arrival as you go along, based on how many miles you have left and the 2 mile per hour rule.

Osmotherley to Clay Bank Top

If you're exhausted, don't climb all of the Cleveland Hills. After the Lord Stones Cafe, as you begin the climb up to the Falconer seat, take the slightly lower path. You can rejoin the hills later on at a stile leading up to the Wainstones, which I strongly recommend you visit. But you can continue on along the lower path to the road at Clay Bank Top.

6

Stepping through the Route

Stepping through the Route

There is a silence about the first couple of days of the Cleveland Way that is profound. It's like stepping back in time. It is easy to imagine that the scene hasn't changed over the centuries. You could be stepping out like the hikers of the 1930s, walking on the same quiet farm roads that even today seem to have little traffic. You hear nothing but the sound of the birds in the trees on these first few days of the walk, as you pass by places with names such as Old Byland and Rievaulx Abbey. You just don't hear quite the same sounds or feel the same sense of timelessness on the Coast-to-Coast Walk or the Pennine Way.

Even though there is now a sculptured Cleveland Way seat, tucked away down a side street as you leave Helmsley, I think the walk gets off to an inauspicious start.

But after some straightforward walking in the environs of Helmsley, you soon get out into the countryside.

Entering a now quiet wood, there was once an Italian prisoner of war camp here. Following paths that rise and fall as they make their way through the trees, there are few signs left of the camp's existence.

Coming out into a clearing, you pass by a very distinctive white-painted lodge, which looks out high above the valley. Beyond it you make your way through more trees and eventually arrive at a road.

Sauntering down the quiet road, you soon pass by Rievaulx Abbey before walking over an ancient packhorse bridge.

Eventually, you leave the road as you turn off towards a gate on your right. Through the gate, a path takes you down to a stream, which flows into the Nettledale Ponds.

If you've settled for a short first day, instead of going to the gate, you should continue on down the bending road towards Scawton. Soon, on your left, you will see the narrow side road which leads to Bungdale Head farm. Simply retrace your steps back to the gate in the morning.

Back on route, you cross via the steppingstones over the stream and then begin to walk alongside a managed plantation. You're looking for a clearing between the trees that has a signpost pointing to it. Climbing up it, you leave the wood and follow a wide track, which eventually leads you to the village of Cold Kirby.

We have sometimes felt quite isolated as we've

made our way up through this clearing in the wood. But then we have often been walking up it as darkness falls, usually at around eight thirty at night. This is when we've been heading for our destination of the Hambleton Inn after making a very late start.

There is a bench in the village of Cold Kirby if you need to take a rest. The houses here are set back from the road and have large front gardens. They always remind me of the well-heeled houses you often see in those American movies.

Beyond Cold Kirby, you walk through an area where there was once an ancient racecourse. There is much evidence of horse training and riding stables around here. Eventually, you come out at the former Hambleton Inn, a place where Cleveland Wayers were once able to camp. It now stands boarded up and almost derelict.

We used to camp at the inn. It was the ideal place to break the first day. Being about 9 miles from Helmsley, you could set off on an afternoon and soon reach here. After putting the tent up, you could enjoy a drink at the bar. Sadly, the inn is no more.

Cutting across the road towards the Glider station on Sutton Bank, you arrive at the escarpment. Standing there admiring the views, on a clear day you can see for miles.

Walking along the cliff edge, you soon arrive at Sutton Bank Visitors Centre. There is a café and toilets here.

Leaving the centre, you return to the escarpment and are soon looking down at Lake Gormire.

Since leaving Helmsley, the walk has gradually been climbing out of the Rye valley as it steadily heads towards the top of the Hambleton Hills.

You're now walking along a clear path by the cliff edge and soon pass by what looks to be a long-since deserted old barn. There is always a strange stillness in the air here, a timelessness. You feel that the scene would be exactly the same if you'd passed by it a hundred years ago.

Continuing on, you arrive at High Paradise Farm, which is about five miles from Sutton Bank. This place is now virtually an outward-bound centre with a café, camping, and many passing walkers.

Beyond High Paradise, you reach the wide Drovers Road and can easily imagine cattle being driven along it.

Following the road, it takes you through a

wood. We once saw animal tracks here in the snow. On coming out at the other side near a gate, there is an ancient stone stuck in the earth. This way marking stone is known as the Steeple Cross. From here, the walk follows for miles alongside a stone boundary wall as it climbs towards the top of Black Hambleton.

From the top of Black Hambleton, you head off down towards the former reservoir at Oakdale. Beyond it, you follow the road into Osmotherley.

The Cleveland Hills stand close to the village of Osmotherley. They are a must, whether you're experiencing them on the Coast-to-Coast, the Lyke Wake Walk, or any other walk.

They are the ultimate walking experience, even if done in thick mist when you could be rubbing shoulders with the spectral Roman armies, which are claimed to have occasionally been seen marching over them.

The Cleveland Hills now also boasts the Lord Stones Café, where refreshments can be bought, which will give you the energy boost needed to see you through the rest of the day.

When you reach the Falconer Seat, think of Pauline and me sitting in it at half-past two in the morning, along with a couple we had met on the

Pennine Way, Andy and Robin.

In a moment of madness, we had agreed to take them on the Lyke Wake Walk. Setting off at the witching hour of midnight, when we eventually reached the Falconer seat and sat down in it, we almost fell asleep.

Both tiredness and the cosiness of four people cramped together on one seat meant that we were soon nodding off. And it took some urging from Andy for us to drag ourselves out of it.

It's a long day to Kildale over the Cleveland Hills. But once you've left them behind and climbed up onto Urra Moor, you soon reach Bloworth Crossing.

Here in a cottage alongside the former railway track, a crossing keeper and his family once lived.

You turn left onto the Cleveland Way path at Bloworth Crossing, and the track over the moors can seem like it's going on forever. Heading off through the heather, there is nothing but wilderness surrounding you. No matter how fast you go, Kildale always seems to be a long time in coming. When you finally reach a gate that takes you off the moors, you breathe a sigh of relief.

You can actually road walk from Great Broughton to Kildale and miss out Urra Moor. But it is satisfying when you finally reach the village and Low Farm, from where you can watch the sun going down over the Cleveland Hills.

If it isn't booked, stay in the farm's bunk barn. It doesn't cost much more than it would to camp there. The bunk barn has a cooker and an electric fire. There is also an old radio, which we've spent many an hour listening to huddled together around the one-bar fire.

Leaving Kildale, you climb up to Captain Cook's monument. We once left a U2 t-shirt hanging off the railings here.

Soon afterwards, you have the opportunity to climb Roseberry Topping and stare back at the Cleveland Hills.

Leaving Roseberry Topping, you're heading for Guisborough Woods. From the high woods, you can take in the views over Guisborough town. It was once easy to get lost in the woods by taking the wrong path. But in recent years, there has been a lot of tree felling, and the dense woods are a lot clearer.

Coming out at Slapewath, backpackers turn right towards the Margrove Camp Site at Boosbeck. This is a friendly site where you can enjoy human company once again, which you may have missed during the first few days of the walk.

The following morning, you can either retrace your steps back to the Hare and Hounds pub at Slapewath to get back on route or follow the road down to Boosbeck village and then get back on track at the village of Skelton.

After making your way through Skelton Green and then through Saltburn's Valley Gardens, you arrive in Saltburn-on-Sea.

Our first impression of Saltburn was that it must have closed down on the outbreak of World War Two and never bothered to reopen.

It was here that I began treating Pauline to toasted sandwiches in local cafés. This was to try to take on board some energy to get us through the rest of the very long day, as we used to walk all the way from Kildale to Staithes.

I also treated Pauline to toasted sandwiches in Whitby and Scarborough and noticed that the price of them got progressively more expensive the further south we went.

Saltburn always seems like such a quiet place with plenty of well-spread shops. You should enjoy some form of sustenance here before heading for Saltburn's seafront and the clifftop.

There is a steep set of steps up the cliff as you climb out of Saltburn. Once you're at the top, you begin to feel on your own again. But from now on, you are likely to keep meeting day walkers who are doing bits of the Cleveland Way.

After a mile along the cliff top, on your right you will see a path off to Brotton. On your left are the plaques urging people not to jump. There is a gentle rise along the cliff top all the way to the 'lucky charm' artwork. Soon afterwards the path begins to go gently downhill, and there are one or two muddy places. You will also see the Skinningrove jetty in the distance. From climbing up the steps at Saltburn to arriving at the beach at Skinningrove, it will take you one hour.

As you near Skinningrove, you will arrive at a Cleveland Way sign. It is the place where you leave the cliffs for a short while. Descend by a series of wooden ladder steps down towards the beach. Try to stay on the path in the sand dunes, you will get sand in your boots as you walk along the beach by the sea.

Arriving at Skinningrove's quaint harbour, here in 1944, some of the Mulberry harbours were moored up, ready for the D-Day landings.

There is a shop somewhere in the village and a

fish and chip shop. There is also a toilet block.

The climb up the double series of steps out of Skinningrove is steep and will take your breath away. But the views back are excellent.

After Skinningrove, the path begins to gradually rise as you head towards the climb over Boulby Cliff. You reach the cliff soon after passing through an isolated farmstead. It will have taken you 45 minutes from Skinningrove to reach the edge of the cliff where the love letter has been carved into the rock, and it will take a further 20 minutes to reach the top of the cliff opposite the television aerial and the nearby trig point. Soon after the summit the path will quickly drop down to the cliff-edge cottages. Then a further long mile of walking will bring you down to the narrow bridge and the quaint seaside village of Staithes.

If you follow the long street that climbs up out of Staithes, you can catch a bus on the main road to Whitby, or you can visit the Coop Supermarket or the fish and chip shop.

You leave Staithes by climbing up from the seafront. The narrow lane out of Staithes is quite steep and I never look forward to it. But on reaching the Cleveland Way sign, the ascent up the cliffside is quite quick. Once you're back on the clifftop, you are only faced by one more really steep climb, and the walk to Runswick Bay is generally easy. It will take you about 85 minutes to walk from Staithes to Runswick Bay.

In terms of escape routes, you pass a path to Hinderwell along the cliff top, and there is also a road up from the hamlet of Port Mulgrave that will take you to Hinderwell in about 10 minutes. This is helpful if you have decided to camp there or wish to get back on the bus route.

Arriving at Runswick Bay, you hope that the sea isn't coming in as you walk for half a mile across the sand before turning up a ravine where you once again begin the climb back onto the top of the cliff. The climb up the cliffside is long and steep via a series of steps. The clifftop path has a slight rise to it all the way to the hamlet of Kettleness. After it, you soon spot the embankment of the old railway line and eventually can look down on this end of the Sandsend railway tunnel. Walking along a path over the top of it, you eventually begin a steep descent via wooden and metal steps down to the other end of the tunnel. From here you follow the old railway track leading towards Sandsend's station house and platform. There you climb down a series of steps into a car park at Sandsend. The journey from Runswick Bay to Sandsend will have taken you about 90 minutes.

Following the seafront, you begin the long road walk into Whitby. Passing by the golf course and numerous memorial seats, you'll eventually arrive at the whalebone arch. Whitby has plenty of shops where you can buy anything you need.

To leave Whitby, you need to climb the infamous series of steps that will take you to the cliff top near Whitby Abbey.

Following the clifftop path, you make your way through a holiday park and then pass Whitby Foghorn station, from where there is a steep climb back up onto the top of the cliff. You soon pass by the caravan park through which walkers on the Coast-to-Coast Walk join the Cleveland Way for the last three miles of their epic journey. You now simply follow the clifftop path all the way along to Robin Hood's Bay. This part of the clifftop is likely to be full of holidaymakers, which makes quite a contrast to the sense of isolation you may have experienced during the early days of the walk.

After Robin Hood's Bay, it begins to become quiet again, but it's hard work as you steadily climb up beyond Boggle Hole and on towards

Ravenscar. Beyond the Visitor Centre shop at Ravenscar the walking becomes easier until you descend to Hayburn Wyke and then climb back out again.

It is really easy to lose the track here as you attempt to climb out of Hayburn Wyke, and you need to be very vigilant.

Beyond it you soon spot Scarborough Castle and keep it in view all the way along the cliff top until you reach this seaside town.

Beyond Scarborough you're back walking on the clifftop path, and you might not meet anyone on it, other than dog walkers, as you make your way towards Filey.

7

Transport Services

Transport Services

Getting There and Back

Arrive at Scarborough by train and then catch a bus to Helmsley from a stop next to the train station. At the end of the walk, you can take a train from Filey to Scarborough, from where you can catch a train to anywhere.

Buses

In the summer there are half hourly buses running all the way down from Saltburn to Whitby. And even out of season, there are hourly buses. So, if you wanted to, you could leave the Cleveland Way path at various places along the coast, such as Saltburn, Staithes, Runswick Bay, Sandsend and travel back and forwards by bus to and from Whitby or any other of the places where the bus stops along the route. The bus you want is the **X4**.

The hourly **X93** bus from Whitby will take you to Robin Hood's Bay and Scarborough.

Buses from Scarborough to Filey and return include the numbers **12/13/555** The Bus from Scarborough to Helmsley is the **128**

Trains

You can catch a train from Filey, which will either take you back to Scarborough or Seamer for trains to York, Leeds, Liverpool.

You can go straight to Hull, where the train will continue on to Doncaster and Sheffield.

Trains from Whitby can take you to Middlesbrough, York, Leeds, Newcastle.

8

Tales for The Tent

Camping in Paradise

When we first walked the Cleveland Way, we used to camp at High Paradise Farm, which was an appropriate place to stay, as it was approximately halfway between Helmsley and Osmotherley.

The farm has since changed hands and today is a hub of walking activity, but back then it was just a couple of farm cottages from where you could fortunately purchase tea and scones.

To attract attention, when you arrived at the farm cottages, you used to ring an old bell, and it is still there today.

Camping was pretty primitive, as you camped on the rough grass opposite the cottages. The loo for campers was a chemical toilet, which was housed under a U-shaped piece of corrugated iron, that looked like a wartime Anderson Shelter.

The farm at that time kept several donkeys who had taken it into their heads that they, too, should use the corrugated iron toilet. In the daylight, the evidence was laid there plain to see. But in the dark, it was like climbing a boulder hill trying to reach the loo.

Mealtimes there were also difficult. The minute you began to cook your tea, you would be surrounded by donkeys who would compete with the farm's hens for a share of your food. After tea, the lazy donkeys would also take to leaning on the tent, and you would be laid there with the constant fear of having a donkey keel over on top of you.

On one occasion, when we were camped there, we heard terrified screams coming from the farm cottage in the middle of the night. The next morning, we learned that someone sleeping there had seen a ghost.

We stayed at the farm during our first attempt at the Cleveland Way. It was late October, and being new to long-distance walking, we were trying to get the most out of the year.

At the time, like a fool, I had devised a way of keeping down the weight in our backpacks. This was achieved by only carrying one sleep mat between us. The idea was that if you placed it sideways, when you slept, it would still support the main parts of your body, mainly your back and backside (it didn't work!). We also carried two cheap sleeping bags.

As the night drew on, we got colder and colder in our sleeping bags and couldn't sleep. In the end, it was so cold that, fully clothed, we tried to sleep back-to-back in one severely stretched sleeping bag, with the other bag spread out over the top of us. But we still couldn't sleep, because it was still so cold.

Then, as dawn began to arrive, we noticed that a leaf pattern had formed on the tent roof. It was late autumn, and we thought that the leaves must have blown off the trees.

But on opening the tent flap, we were amazed to find that it had snowed during the night and there was a total whiteout. A snow blizzard was raging, and, apart from the intense cold and a strong wind blowing the tent all night, we had been totally unaware of it.

Getting up, we were a little bit afraid, as we had 8 miles to trek across the open moor to Osmotherley and had never walked this route before.

The terrible snowstorm didn't' look like it was abating, and we were half hoping that the farmer would take pity on us and give us a lift into Osmotherley. But he went off to work just as though it was business as usual. Luckily, our OS map showed that the route for most of the walk was across open moor alongside a stone wall.

It was clear that the snowstorm wasn't going to stop, and, sitting in the tent, we were simply getting colder and colder. So, we put on every item of clothing we had and, in the swirling snow, took down and packed the soaking wet tent. Then, like two Arctic explorers, we set off into the blizzard.

Just after High Paradise, you come to an old drove road, which shortly leads you into a wood. The wind howled on the drove road, and the snow hurtled down. Everything was solid white. On entering the wood, the wind dropped a little. There was snow hanging on the trees, and the paths were completely covered. We forgot the weather for a moment as it was so enchanting, just like the pictures in a Rupert Bear annual. In the snow on the path, we began to notice tracks made by some animal that must have recently passed that way. The sight was amazing and true to life; we never had a camera with us to record it!

We soon left the forest behind and made our way across the moor. The snow continued to come down, and everything was a total whiteout.

The howling wind was coming from the west, and the left-hand sides of our bodies were soon totally wet and frozen. But committed, side-by-side, we plodded on through the blizzard and met no one.

After about three hours of steady walking, we passed the summit of Black Hambleton and began the descent towards the Osmotherley reservoir.

As we neared the bottom of the hill, we were amazed to find that not only did the snow blizzard suddenly stop, but on the lower ground there wasn't a drop of snow to be seen.

Eventually, soaking wet, we arrived in Osmotherley. Sitting in various pubs and cafes, we tried in vain to dry ourselves. But it was to no avail, as we were just so wet. Eventually, we had no choice but to abandon the walk and call a friend to come and pick us up.

The worst thing was that nobody in the village believed us when we told them that it had been snowing.

The Railway Age

There used to be a fantastic railway line that ran all the way from Scarborough to Whitby, Sandsend and beyond. It followed the coastline for much of the way.

You can imagine how brilliant it would have been to be able to look out of the train carriage windows at places such as Sandsend and see the sea. Or travel through the pitch-black tunnels that were dug through the sea cliffs and which you now walk over. Today, they stand disused and empty.

If you go on YouTube, you can see a great video of two 'urban explorers' walking through the abandoned Sandsend railway tunnel in the pitch black, from one creepy end to the other.

There is also a great video showing the east coastline from Scarborough to Sandsend before it was closed. And you can, for example, see how Ravenscar and many of the other small railway stations once looked, including the fantastic steel viaduct at Sandsend.

You can still stand on the old station platform at Ravenscar and imagine how, 50 years ago, you could have caught a train from there to Robin Hood's Bay and Scarborough.

The cinder-track of the old Scarborough/Whitby

railway line is still there. And there are places on the Cleveland Way where, as an alternative, you can follow it, such as from Robin Hood's Bay to Ravenscar and from Hayburn Wyke into Scarborough. We have occasionally done this to vary the route, but it always seems to be so much longer. Beyond Ravenscar, it is also difficult to rejoin the main route.

Skinningrove

Skinningrove was once a small fishing community. Today, although beginning to look better than it did, it still looks like a run-down place with its old pigeon lofts and ore-coloured becks.

In the early days when we did the walk, it also had male residents, who, when you passed by them on the seafront, looked at you strangely, as if to say, 'We've got strangers in the village!' You'd half turn to see if there was a banjo player sitting strumming on the quayside.

The seafront today looks as though it has been done up a bit, and some of the terraced houses have become holiday homes.

From a once rundown community, Skinningrove is beginning to look like a cheap place to bag a holiday home with great views of the sea and its own beach.

Seafront Buildings

A macabre but interesting feature to look out for in each of the towns and villages along the East Coast are some small 19th-century seafront buildings. Built not much bigger than the size of a garage, they once served as mortuaries for washed-up seafarers. You can spot them in Saltburn, Staithes, Whitby, Scarborough, and Filey. Indeed, the path you're following along the cliff top will be the same one that sailors once followed when trying to pick up a ship in Whitby or other small ports along the Northeast coast.

The Walkers Halt on Boulby Cliff

The Walker's Halt was one of a row of cottages situated high on Boulby Cliff overlooking the sea. You would pass it as you began to make your way down off the cliff towards Staithes.

A retired professional couple used to live there, and they would make refreshments and snacks for passing walkers.

The husband was infamous for being willing to prick any blisters you might have, a service for which there was no charge!

The couple loved having walkers sit in their living room and would chat with them at any time of the day or night. Stopping there provided us with the energy we drastically needed after a long day's walk from Kildale, before the final long mile down into Staithes. Sadly, the couple are no longer with us. But as you near Staithes, walking in along the cliff top, keep your eyes peeled for the rather grand-looking memorial seat dedicated to them. It bears their name and that of their former home, 'Walkers Halt.' So, their history lives on.

The Wainstones

When you arrive at the Wainstones and climb your weary way onto the top of them, take a closer look at the gigantic stone slabs you're sitting on. Notice the hundreds of initials that walkers have carved on these rocks over the years. On the very top stones you may even see mine, the RM, which I carved on them back in 1975, when I was having my first punishing taste of the North York Moors, on the Lyke Wake Walk. Pauline subsequently added her initials to the same spot many years later. If you look to your right, you will also see two large flat slabs of stone on the very edge of the Wainstones, which have a gap between them. I stood astride these as the sun slowly began to rise up on the horizon on a June morning in 1975.

Tanned in March

We often attempted the Cleveland Way in early spring, especially if we were doing the Coast-to-Coast walk in the summer.

Once we started the Cleveland Way towards the end of March, and every morning, we'd wake up to frost on the tent and yet the sun shining. By the time we packed up the tent and continued our walk over the moors, the sun would be beating down on us.

When I returned to work the following week, I was as brown as a berry, and my students kept asking me which tropical country I'd spent my Easter holiday in. Was it the Canary Islands, Tenerife? Few of them believed that I got the tan walking on the North York Moors.

The sad thing about that walk was that every day, as we walked over the moors and sea cliffs in glorious weather, I recorded it on my video camera. Arriving back home, I put the walk tape into my VCR, ready to enjoy reliving it all over again. Then Pauline and I went and prepared a bit of supper to eat while we watched it. Unbeknownst to us, while we were doing this, our son was busy recording a football match over the tape, and so we never got to see it.

A Love Letter on Boulby Cliff

As you near the rocky outcrops on the edge of Boulby Cliff, keep your eyes peeled for an inscription that someone has carved into the cliff face.

A man, so much in love with his recently departed wife, once stood there and diligently chiselled a love letter into the rock.

It must have taken him hours, but it stands as a testament of his love for her, which in these seemingly transient times, really should be admired.

The climb up from Clay Bank Top onto Urra Moor

Comet Hale-Bopp

Once, in the early hours of the morning, while Pauline and I were camped at Trigpoint 49 at Staithes, we awoke to see a huge comet in the night sky. It was so bright and had come so close to the earth that it could be clearly seen. The view from our tent at Staithes was phenomenal. I had my video camera in the tent, but sad to say, I was too tired to record this one-off event for posterity and sadly went back to sleep.

Gorse Busters

After leaving Runswick Bay, you walk for half a mile along the beach before turning right up a narrow ravine that has a beck running down the middle of it. When the tide rises, it also has the North Sea flowing up it. Once the sea starts coming in, it used to be difficult to get from one side of the ravine to the other, where you need to be. Today a wooden bridge has been put there to enable you to get across.

On one of our early walks, with the water in the beck widening, we couldn't find a place narrow enough to get safely across. So, we considered that the best thing to do was to climb up along the side of the ravine to get further along it and then to climb back down when we spotted a narrower place to cross the beck. This we did, but still couldn't see anywhere suitable to cross. So, we decided to climb even higher along the side of the ravine in the hope that we could eventually spot a place to cross.

Unfortunately, we then began to have to fight our way through thick gorse bushes. These tore at the flesh on our bare arms and legs, and we eventually reached a point where we considered that it would be too painful to make our way back down again. So, we decided that we had no choice but to continue on to the top of the ravine with the hope that there would be easier walking.

This proved to be a huge mistake. The gorse bushes became thicker and thicker, and our flesh began to become even more scratched. We desperately needed to get out of the gorse, as it was also becoming impossible to see where we were putting our feet. Then above us we spotted the roof of an abandoned WW2 concrete pillbox hidden amongst the undergrowth and we slowly climbed up towards it. Badly scratched, we eventually managed to climb onto the concrete top of the pillbox.

We must have been the first people to have done this since the end of the war. Standing there, looking around us, we were marooned, totally surrounded by gorse bushes. It then dawned on me that we also couldn't be seen and nobody would know that we were up there. For the first time in my life, I felt like shouting, "Help!"

Surveying the way ahead, nothing could be seen but thick gorse. There was no way we could continue on, and so must go back down the way we came. Taking a deep breath, we began our descent. Due to the incline of the ravine, the only safe way through the gorse was on our backsides. Leaning backwards on our hands, we slid slowly down, fearing at any moment that we would disappear beneath the gorse. Slowly and painfully, we edged our way towards the bottom of the ravine. Despite picking up even more bleeding scratches and ripped skin, particularly on the backs of our legs, we eventually arrived at the bottom of the ravine. There we had no alternative but to wade across the beck before following a path up the other side of the ravine that led up to the top of the cliff. Looking back across the ravine, we could see we had made the correct decision in retracing our footsteps. The cliff top opposite was covered in gorse bushes for as far as the eyes could see.

Lyke Wake Walkers

When you're out on the Cleveland Hills, spare a thought for the 100,000 or more Lyke Wake Walkers who once passed this way. A 40-mile-long trek across the North York Moors, the Lyke Wake Walk was a challenge that had to be completed within 24 hours.

The walk accompanies you all the way from Osmotherley to Bloworth Crossing. When you turn off from there towards Kildale, Lyke Wake walkers are still less than halfway through their trek. It is genuinely a walk in which you can start to feel your body slowly disintegrating.

9

Joining it all together

The Tabular Hills Walk

The Tabular Hills Walk or Missing Link

If you've left your car parked in Helmsley or have a further three days to spare, then you can now turn the Cleveland Way into a circular route.

The official end of the Cleveland Way is at Filey, but if after sitting on the completion stone above Filey Brigg, you feel that you have any energy left. Then you can continue on down from the clifftop to Filey station and catch the train to Scarborough. Then, after shopping for groceries, make your way back to the seafront and walk to the end of the North Bay at Scalby Mills. (You can catch a bus there).

At the Old Scalby Mills Pub, retrace your steps back over the metal bridge and up onto the clifftop. In about five minutes of walking along it, you'll come to a sign that points the way across a field in the direction of Helmsley.

Follow the sign and you'll soon arrive at a road and back at the Scarborough Caravan and Camping site where you probably spent last night and where, if you were wise, you probably left your tent and backpack before you walked to Filey. Spend the night here; the site also has its own pub. The next day you can begin your trip back to Helmsley via the Tabular Hill's route:

Itinerary
Tabular Hills Walk
Scarborough to Helmsley 48 miles

Day 1 Scalby Mills - Hole of Holcum
16 miles

Day 2 Hole of Holcum - Newton on Rawcliffe
9 miles

Day 3 Newton on Rawcliffe - Hutton le Hole
9 miles

Day 4 Hutton le Hole - Helmsley 13.5 miles

After roughing it at the various campsites on the Cleveland Way, the campsites along the Tabular Hills walk are all of good quality. There isn't a campsite at Helmsley, but there are plenty on the way back into Scarborough by bus.

If you're not got the time to do it this year, then consider doing the Missing Link or Tabular Hills walk next year.

It takes four days to complete the walk, and you could spend the first night at the Scarborough campsite.

Leaving Scarborough, the camping is as follows:

Day 1
Camp at Marfit Head Farm
Saltersgate
Pickering
North Yorkshire
YO18 7NR
Tel: 01751 460415
Details: Turn left as you arrive on the busy A169 Pickering to Whitby road. Walk all the way through the car Park and continue on along the grass verge. Within 5 minutes you will come to the entrance to the campsite. This is a good campsite with hot water, a washroom and pot washing facilities.

Day 2
Bank Top Camping
Low Moor Road
Pickering
North Yorkshire
Tel: 07771 911039
Details: This is a nice airy campsite, washroom, trees.

Day 3

Hutton Le Hole Caravan Park

Westfield Lodge,
Hutton le Hole,
North Yorkshire,
YO62 6UG
Tel: 01751 417261
Email: huttonleholecaravanpark@hotmail.com
Details: Try not to arrive there on a weekend, let them know that you're doing the Tabular Hills walk. Lots of facilities on the site.

Details

On the Final day, take the bus into Scarborough from Helmsley and catch the train home. Or, if you want to camp, stop off at one of the campsites you'll see from the bus, or return to the Scarborough campsite.